Let's Play

Puppets Tell Parables

Parables of Jesus, retold by Gina Hall

Illustrated by Finola Stack

A Redemptorist Publication

Published by Redemptorist Publications in 2007
A registered Charity limited by guarantee.
Registered in England 3261721

Illustrations: Finola Stack
Design: Rosemarie Pink

First published in August 2007

ISBN 978-0-85231-339-8

Printed by Polar Group Limited Leicester LE4 9TZ

Redemptorist
PUBLICATIONS
Alphonsus House Chawton Hampshire GU34 3HQ
Telephone 01420 88222 Fax 01420 88805
rp@rpbooks.co.uk www.rpbooks.co.uk

CONTENTS

INTRODUCTION

Help! How can I teach Bible stories to pre-school-age children and entertain them at the same time?

There are increasing numbers of churches and individuals who want to involve their young children in some kind of Christian teaching. This booklet provides ten complete puppet shows teaching the parables of Jesus. These can be used at home or in groups. You could use them in school, nursery or playgroup. You could use them for teaching in any children's church group (for example Sunday School, Children's Liturgy or a Family Service), or you could develop a whole service around the puppet shows for use in church worship. You can also make a great children's presentation using the puppets!

The material is aimed primarily at two- to five-year-olds, but also works well with children up to the age of ten. You don't need to have any biblical knowledge – the book tells you everything you need to know to get across the point of each parable. You don't need to spend ages preparing things either. After all, we're not all cut out to be *Blue Peter* presenters! One person can present the whole puppet show, but if you're using the puppets as part of a service or assembly you might want some help in organising the children.

Alternatively, if you are using the puppets with a mixed-age group, the older children could be involved in the "performance". They could work the puppets as a presentation either for younger children or for a church congregation or small group. Once you have started using the puppets the possibilities are endless – and so is the fun!

The puppets you need for each story are printed in the book, ready for you to trace, or to photocopy. You're not restricted to using the scripts with puppets – you could simply tell them as stories or act them out as dramas. You can use them with older children and get the children involved in putting on the show. This works really well as a children's presentation; just make sure you have a good narrator, and don't worry if the puppets appear at the wrong time – no one will mind and the audience will love the show! Make the puppets larger by enlarging them as you photocopy them if you are presenting a show in a larger space and the children can be behind a large fabric drape above which the puppets perform as on a stage. You could always make your own puppets too.

You can use the puppet scripts as "read to me" stories at home. Children could use their own toys or dolls as the puppets, or cut out and make the puppets in the book.

If you use the puppets you will find that children and their parents are fascinated by this method of telling the Bible. Children as young as two will be totally absorbed in even the most basic puppet figures and the messages are simple enough for them to understand and relate to their own lives. Each story includes an idea for a short prayer. There is also a "Nutshell" which gives a brief explanation of the theme of the parable; a "Chatter Box" time, which gives a few questions for the children to use to relate the story to their lives; and "Something to Do", which suggests a follow-up activity. If you want to read the stories in their original context, the Bible reading references are given at the top of each story. You might find it helpful to read them before you start your presentation but you don't have to.

Setting the Stage

1. The theatre. This can be as simple or as complex as you choose to make it, but some kind of stage makes all the difference to your puppet show. The simplest stage can be made using a large cardboard box. Turn it open-end down and decorate the front side with coloured paper. Your puppets can then perform on top of the front edge and you can rest your script on the box.

If you are a capable woodworker or feel more adventurous you could make a stage using plywood or medium-density fibreboard with wooden supports. You might even find a puppet theatre in a toy shop which would suit your purpose.

2. The puppets. All the puppets you need are included in this book. You can either photocopy them or trace them onto card. Then colour in. The colouring could be done with your pre-school children, perhaps as a before-the-show activity or as part of a home and family time. If you colour in before the puppet show, make sure you have a few spares and some sticky tape for emergency repairs! Once you have coloured them, simply mount onto folded card sticks, lolly sticks or thin bamboo canes. The card needs to be stiff enough to support the puppets, and you can attach the sticks using staples, glue or tape.

Each puppet show includes one puppet which you can use for a short "make" with your children. This involves a sticking and gluing activity, which is always really popular! The "make" shouldn't take long and needn't be too messy. Use a plastic sheet on the floor or table and pre-glue the puppet with PVA or a glue stick. Then the children can stick on the covering – for example feathers for the birds in "The Sower", chopped-up knitting wool for the donkey in "The Good Samaritan". A lot of the stories include an option for all the children to have a puppet, such as a bird or a donkey or some money. The children can then be really involved in the story – and have something to take home.

3. Putting on the show. Now you have the theatre and the puppets, so you're ready to do the show. Encourage the children to sit down at eye level to the top of your stage. This might be on the floor. If you're in a church or chapel you might find kneelers to sit on, or a section of carpet. This helps create a space in which the children feel a bit contained, which can be helpful to you in keeping them all together and not running about! Have your script where you can refer to it comfortably. The whole script is printed together with the stage directions telling you which puppet you need and what to do with them – don't worry if you don't follow the exact directions and it's quite OK to ad lib. The whole show will take four to six minutes.

4. After the show. If you are using the puppets as teaching for a school or church group it can be useful to display them afterwards. They make a great wall display, and people can see what you have been doing, and how the puppets are constructed. A decorative "theatre" can be a good way to do this.

For your wall display - make a cut-out theatre to frame your puppets.

Colour in the curtains and staple to the pinboard.

You can fix the puppets to the display and write a short text to go with them explaining what the story was about. For example: "Today our puppets told the story of the Sower, and we learned…" – here you can write the "Nutshell" found at the end of each section. This is the basic teaching "in a nutshell" that you are telling through the puppet show.

Parables

So, what are parables? Your older children or parents may be interested to know this.
Parables are a special way that Jesus used to teach people about God, about heaven and about how we should live our lives. They are stories which the people listening to could easily understand and relate to the world they knew. For example, in the parable of the Sower, Jesus talks about seeds and how well they grow. His audience knew all about growing crops, so that helped them to learn about faith in God.

Bright Ideas for "Wraparound" Material!

The puppet shows are intended to have a flexible use. You can use them at home, or in a small group at school or nursery, or as part of a children's church activity or church teaching group. You could build a complete children's worship time around the puppet show, just by adding some prayers and some songs.

Prayers with the Puppets

Praying with children can be really special, both in family prayer time and in bigger groups. Keep the prayers short and simple and let the children get involved. You can use the ideas from the puppet show as a starting point and lead into more general prayers. These can be under the headings of "please" and "thank you". Everyone in the group can add things they would like to ask God for ("please") and things they want to say "thank you" to God for. You might also want to say the Lord's Prayer together.

Songs with the Puppets

Children love to sing, and the puppet stories can be made even more fun by adding an appropriate song or two. There are lots of good songs and good books of songs. You can liven things up even more by adding actions to the songs – make use of the puppets too!

The Lost Sheep

(Luke 15:1-7)

Cast

Shepherd • Flock of sheep • Mountain • Valley • Shepherd's group of friends • Single sheep - ***this can be the "make". Stick cotton wool to make the fleece. Alternatively you can make sheep for all the children, which can be the flock. They can take them home later.***

Stage directions

The Lost Sheep

This is a story Jesus told so that people could learn what God is like.

1. Shepherd, flock of sheep and single sheep come onstage, they all walk about and huddle together.

There was once a shepherd who had one hundred sheep (1). What a lot of sheep, "baa, baa, baa". Every day he counted all the sheep to make sure they were all there: "1, 2, 3, 4... 98, 99, 100". He was very good at counting!

2. Shepherd and flock remain, but the single sheep wanders offstage.

(2) One day when he counted them: "1, 2, 3, 4... 98, 99... 99? Only 99?" He counted them all again to make sure: "1, 2, 3, 4... 98, 99". Still only 99!

3. Shepherd walks away from flock, and the flock move offstage.

Oh dear. One of his sheep was definitely missing. So the shepherd left the ninety-nine sheep (3), and he searched and he searched and he searched for the lost sheep.

4. Shepherd walks and looks, the valley moves onstage (as though the shepherd is walking past it).

5. Shepherd keeps walking and looking and the mountain moves onstage (as though the shepherd is walking past it).

He looked in the valleys (4) and he looked on the mountains (5) – he looked here and there and everywhere. He looked behind bushes, he looked behind rocks. He looked near and he looked far away.

6. Single sheep comes onstage. Shepherd "finds" the single sheep, and carries it.

7. Shepherd and single sheep are joined by the flock.

He didn't stop looking until at last he found the lost sheep (6). "There you are," he said when he found it, "what are you doing all alone here?" And he carried it back to the other ninety-nine sheep (7).

8. Shepherd and the sheep are joined by his friends.

9. Shepherd jumps up and down.

10. Shepherd, all sheep and friends onstage and all jump up and down.

The lost sheep was pleased and the other ninety-nine sheep were pleased and the shepherd was pleased. He was so pleased that he called all his friends and neighbours (8). He was so pleased that he jumped up and down (9); he was so pleased that he gave a big party for all his friends and neighbours (10). And they were all pleased too!

Nutshell

God is like that shepherd. When we stray away from God, God just wants us to come back and tries to find us all the time. And God is so pleased when we do come back!

Chatter Box

Have you ever lost something and then found it again?

How did you feel when you found it?

Have you ever got lost?

Do you know how your mum or dad felt when they couldn't find you?

Prayer Time

We thank you, Lord, that you care so much about us that you search for us when we are lost.
We pray for anyone who feels lost, that they will feel safe and know that God loves them.

Something to Do

Try counting the biggest flock of sheep you can find. It's not easy; they keep moving!

Fold here
Strengthen with folded card, pasted on reverse

Fold here
Strengthen with folded card pasted on reverse
Fold here
Strengthen with folded card pasted on reverse

The Good Samaritan

(Luke 10:30-37)

Cast

Man in robe • Same man without robe • Robbers • Priest • Levite • Samaritan • Donkey ***(this can be the "make" - stick on chopped-up brown wool for fur; you could make a donkey for each child).***

The Good Samaritan

Stage directions

Jesus told this story to the people.

1. Well-dressed man enters looking around and walking.

A man set out on a journey from Jerusalem to Jericho (1). He was worried about the journey because the road went through dangerous places where bad people and robbers and muggers lived. So as he walked along he looked this way and that way, he looked in front and looked behind, and he didn't like it.

He walked on a little further, and he kept looking this way and that way, he looked in front and looked behind, and he didn't like it.

2. Robbers rush forward shouting "arhhh", "grrhh" (etc.).

3. Robbers beat the man, he fights back and shouts, "help! help!" Robbers hit him, he falls down. He gets up, they hit him again. He gets up, they hit him, he falls.

4. The robbers run away – replace man-in-robe puppet with beaten up man-in-rags puppet lying onstage.

He walked on and suddenly there was a lot of shouting and noise (2). The man was being attacked by robbers. He struggled and kicked out, he wriggled and shouted (3), but the robbers were big and strong and they hit the poor man. They stole his money and his clothes and everything he had, and they ran away and left him (4).

5. Man-in-rags lying onstage, groaning.

The man felt terrible (5). He lay by the road for ages. After a long time, a priest came along the road

6. Priest walks along, looking around, he sees the man, and walks across the stage keeping his distance from the man-in-rags.

(6) – he worked in the Temple. The priest didn't like the road, because it was dangerous with robbers and muggers; he looked this way and that way, in front and behind. He saw the man. "Oh good," thought the man, "this priest will help me." But the priest didn't help the man. He walked on along the road, along the other side of the road. The poor man felt terrible.

Eventually the poor man heard someone else coming along the road. It was a Levite (7) – that's someone else who worked in the Temple. The Levite didn't like the road either; he looked this way and that way, he looked in front and behind. He saw the man. "Oh good," thought the man, "this Levite will help me." But the Levite didn't help the man. He walked on along the road, along the other side of the road. The poor man felt terrible.

7. Levite walks along, looking around, he sees the man-in-rags, and walks on, keeping his distance.

The man lay for ages by the side of the road. When along the road came a Samaritan (8) with his donkey. He didn't like the road, he looked this way and

8. Samaritan with donkey onstage walk along, both looking around.

that way, he looked in front and he looked behind, he patted his donkey. "Oh dear," thought the man, "this Samaritan won't help me. People like me don't mix with Samaritans, and Samaritans don't mix with people like me." He felt terrible.

But the Samaritan didn't walk by. He was kind to the man and he bandaged his cuts and bruises. The man felt much better. The Samaritan put him on his donkey (9) and took him to an inn. And he told the people at the inn to take care of the man until he was better. He even left enough money to pay for everything the man needed.

9. Samaritan moves to the man and lifts the man onto the donkey.

When Jesus told this story he asked the people: "Who was kind to the man who was robbed and left all cut and bruised by the roadside?
Do you think it was the priest (10)?
Or the Levite (11)?
Or the Samaritan (12)?"

10. Priest (all say "No").

11. Levite (all say "No").

12. Samaritan (all say "Yes!").

Jesus wants us to be like the Samaritan and to help other people, even if they're people we don't really like!

Nutshell

God wants us to care about each other and not to be mean to people because they are different from us.

Chatter Box

Has someone helped you when you were hurt or afraid?

Have you ever helped someone else who was hurt or afraid?

Do you think that you would help someone who wasn't your friend?

Prayer Time

Thank you for people who help us when we are in trouble. Please help us to help other people, even if we don't like them.

Something to Do

Find out about a charity that helps people who are very different from you.

Lollystick will
fit here
and here.

The Big Party

(Luke 14:16-24)

Cast

King • King's son • Servant • The king's friends x 3 • People in the street • Food - ***this can be the "make". Use cut-out pictures of food to stick onto the puppet - everyone can have a food puppet.***

The Big Party

Stage directions

Jesus told this story to teach people more about heaven.

1. King walks onstage and paces to and fro.

2. King is joined by his son and they walk together.

3. Servant enters and bows to the king.

4. Food appears.
5. Clear stage.

There was once a king (1) and he wanted to give a great big enormous party, a banquet, a feast, a wonderful, special do for his son's wedding (2).
So he started to get everything ready. He asked his servant (3) to clean the house, and he asked his cook to cook lots of special food. There were meats and pies and fruits and cakes and lots of delicious things (4). Yum, yum, yum (5).

Then the king sent his servant to ask all his friends to come to the party.
"Come to the king's party, his feast, his wonderful, special do to celebrate his son's wedding. There are meats and pies and fruits and cakes, and lots of delicious things," the servant said.

6. Servant and first friend go onstage, the servant bows. The first friend goes offstage.

But the king's friends did not come to the party.
(6) "Oh, I'm too busy," said one, "I must go to my fields."

7. The second friend comes onstage and the servant bows to him. The second friend goes offstage.

8. The third friend comes onstage and the servant bows to him. The third friend beats the servant, who falls down, groaning. Third friend goes offstage.

(7) "Oh, I'm too busy," said another, "I must go to work."

Some of the king's friends didn't just say, "I'm too busy" - they got into a rage and beat the king's servant (8).

9. King onstage joined by the limping servant who bows (slowly), they talk.

10. The food puppet appears.

11. King and food puppet go offstage.

12. Servant walks along and is joined by the group of street people, they talk, street people jump up and down. The king, his son, and the food puppet come onstage.

That was very bad. So the servant came back and told the king, (9) and the king said to his servant, "My party, my banquet, my feast, my wonderful special do is all ready, (10) there are meats and pies and fruits and cakes and lots of delicious things, and my friends will not come! They do not deserve to come, they have been rude and they have beaten my servant. Go into the streets and invite all the people you find there, the good and the bad, the rich and the poor." (11) So the servant went out and invited all the people he found (12), and all these people came and the king's house was full.

It really was a great banquet, a smashing feast and altogether a very special do. The king walked among his guests, the good and the bad, the rich and poor whom his servant had asked to the party. And the guests thanked the king for inviting them to such a wonderful party.

Nutshell

God invites us all to his party in heaven, but some people refuse the invitation and some people are cold-hearted and mean and will not go.

Chatter Box

Do you think the king's friends had good reasons for not coming to the party?

How do you think he felt when they wouldn't come?

Have you ever asked some of your friends to a party and they didn't come? Did that make you feel a bit sad?

Prayer Time

We thank you, Lord, for the invitation to join you in your heavenly party.
Help us to come to you with warm hearts, and to say, "yes please" to you.

Something to Do

Have a party and ask a few people who are not your best friends.

Fold here
Strengthen with folded card pasted on reverse

The Wise and Foolish Builders

(Luke 6:46-49)

Cast

First man • Second man • Rocks • Half-built house • Finished house - ***this can be the "make". Use cut-out paper squares for bricks and tiles.*** **• Sand • Second house • Fallen house • Rain -** ***you can use the puppet in the book or make your own: this could be made of cut-up silver shreds or foil. You can sprinkle this around if a lot of mess isn't a problem.***

The Wise and Foolish Builders

Stage directions

This is a story Jesus told people so that they would know how to live good lives.

There were once two men (1) and they each decided to build a house (2).

1. The two men walk onstage.

2. The second man walks offstage.

The first man (3) found a nice place to build his house. It had good views, it was near a stream for water and it was sheltered from the wind. It was the perfect spot (4). So he started to work. It was hard work - he had to dig into the rock to make a strong base for his house. He dug and he dug and he dug. "Phew, this is hard work," he panted, and on he went. He dug and he dug and he dug with his shovel. He used his pickaxe - bash, bash, bash.

3. The first man looks around. The rock puppet comes onstage as though he is walking towards it.

4. Then the first man moves over to the rocks.

After a while he had made a really good base and so he started to build his house (5).

He carried bricks and stone, he built up the walls.

5. The half-built house appears from the back of the stage.

"Phew, this is hard work," he panted. He built and he built and he built. He built good strong walls. Then he carried wood and tiles for the roof. "Phew, this is hard work," he panted. But then the roof was on, the house was finished (6), and he moved in straight away (7).

6. The finished house replaces the half-finished one.

7. The man looks at the house and goes inside (behind the house). Move house and man offstage.

Now the second man (8) came to build his house. He didn't like the idea of all the hard work it took to make a base with all that digging and bashing and panting.

8. The second man walks onstage and looks for a place to build.

"I'll make my house here on this nice soft sand (9). That will be much easier," he said. So he did just that. He got on very quickly, and soon his house was finished (10). He moved in straight away.

9. The sand puppet appears.

10. The second house appears from the back of the stage – the man goes inside.

(11) Now both men were sitting in their new houses when it started to rain (12) and it rained and it rained and it rained. There were torrents and torrents and torrents of water coming down.

11. Both finished houses and men onstage (in their houses).

12. The rain falls on both houses – use the rain puppet or cut-up silver shreds (get someone else to do the rain if you want to manage both houses throughout).

13. The second man's house starts to shake.

14. The second man runs out of his house.

15. Replace the house on the sand with the fallen house.

The first man who had worked so hard to build his house on the rock sat inside and he was warm and dry. His house stood firm and solid. But the second man, the one who had built on the sand, sat and felt worried. At first a little rain came in underneath the walls of his house, then the house shook (13), then more rain came in, then the house began to slide over the sand. Out ran the man (14). The house quivered, it shook, it rocked and then down it came KER SPLAT! (15)

Jesus told people that they needed to build their lives on God, and that is like the wise builder building on rock. If we don't build our lives on God, when hard times come, we will be like the man in the house built on sand and we won't be able to cope with the hard times.

Nutshell

If we build our lives on God we will be secure and able to deal with difficult things.

Chatter Box

Have you ever made a house out of building blocks or Lego®?

Have you noticed that it stands up better if you take more time and effort to make it? Does it feel good when you work hard at something?

Prayer Time

We thank you, Lord, for sending your Son, Jesus, to teach us how to build our lives on you. We pray that you will always help us to build our lives on you.

Something to Do

Build a house with Lego® or bricks - try and make a really good, strong house that won't fall down too easily.

Fold here
Strengthen with folded card pasted on reverse

Fold here
Strengthen with folded card pasted on reverse

Fold here Strengthen with folded card pasted on reverse

Fold here Strengthen with folded card pasted on reverse
Fold here Strengthen with folded card pasted on reverse

The Rich Fool

(Luke 12:13-21)

Cast

Jesus • Group • Young man • Rich man • Fields • Barns (old) • Workmen • Barns (new) • Crops - ***this is the "make". Stick cut-out pictures of vegetables, corn, straw etc. onto the puppet; each child can have one and be involved in the show.***

The Rich Fool

Stage directions

1. Jesus walks onstage with the group of people and the young man.

2. Young man puppet moves forward.

3. All go offstage.

4. The rich man walks onstage.

5. The field puppet comes across, entering from the other end of the stage.

6. He continues to walk and the fields are replaced with the barns.

(1) One day Jesus was teaching when someone in the crowd (2) said, "Hey, Jesus, my brother has taken all the family money, and he won't give me my share. It's so unfair! Will you tell him to give me my share?" So Jesus told this story to help all the people understand that being greedy and having lots of stuff is not good (3).

There was a rich man (4). He had a big farm with lots of fields (5). The fields had good soil, so the crops grew very well. So the rich man grew even richer, and he was very pleased. And he looked at all his crops and felt very happy. Then he looked at his barns (6) and he was not very happy. "My barns are too small to hold all the crops that I have grown. This is no good! How can I eat and drink and relax and be happy, when I cannot keep all the crops I can grow?"

So he thought, and he looked at his barns, and he

thought some more. He scratched his head and he paced about. Then at last he said: "I know what I will do. I will pull down these barns, and then I will build new barns – bigger barns that will hold all my crops."

7. Workmen join the rich man in front of the barns, then the rich man walks off.

8. The workmen knock down the barns, which go down the back of the stage.

9. The new barns puppet comes up onstage.

10. The rich man joins the workmen in front of the barns. Then the workmen leave.

11. The crops appear with the rich man and the barns, he looks at them and walks up and down.

So he called in his workmen (7). "Pull down these barns", he said, "and build me bigger, better barns." So the workmen set to work – bang, crash, bash they went, and they did pull down the old barns (8). Then the workmen set to work again – hammer, saw, nail they went. And up went (9) the new bigger, better barns. The rich man (10) looked at the new, bigger, better barns and he felt very happy. Now he filled the new barns with the crops (11).

"There, now I can store all my crops. I can eat and drink and relax, and look at my big barns full of my crops. Yes! My crops – mine, all mine! Ah, this is what is important to me – having lots of good things, lots of great stuff."

God looked at the rich man and was sad, and God said to the man, "You fool! All this stuff is not important. Faith and love are important. When you die, all the stuff will belong to other people, but your faith and love will be with you for ever. Faith and love are the best things, the richest things, and stuff is not important at all!"

It was too late for the rich man to learn that faith and love were more important than stuff, because that very night he died (12).

12. Then the man, the barns and the crops go offstage.

13. Jesus and the group and the young man walk onstage.

(13) Jesus looked at the young man who wanted his share of the family money.

"You see, money is not important - what you own, or what you can buy is not important. But if you make those things important, you will become greedy. If you are greedy then you will lose your faith in God and your love for God and for other people."

"Yes, well that's all very well," said the young man, "but it's my money and anyway, if I don't get it how will I get food and clothes and things like that?"

Jesus said, "You should not worry about those things. Trust God and he will care for you always. Have faith and love, and you will be richer than the richest man with his crops and his big barns."

Nutshell

God tells us that things are not important. If we make them important in our lives then they may become more important to us than faith and love. Faith and love are very important.

Chatter Box

Do you like having a lot of things like toys and treats?

Do you think those things are important?

Do you know anyone who is really greedy and doesn't like to share?

Do you enjoy playing with them?

Prayer Time

Thank you, God, that you give us the things we need. Help us to share our good things with other people and not to be greedy.

Something to Do

Sort out some toys you don't want any more (with Mum or Dad to help you) and give them to charity.

Fold here
Strengthen with folded card
pasted on reverse

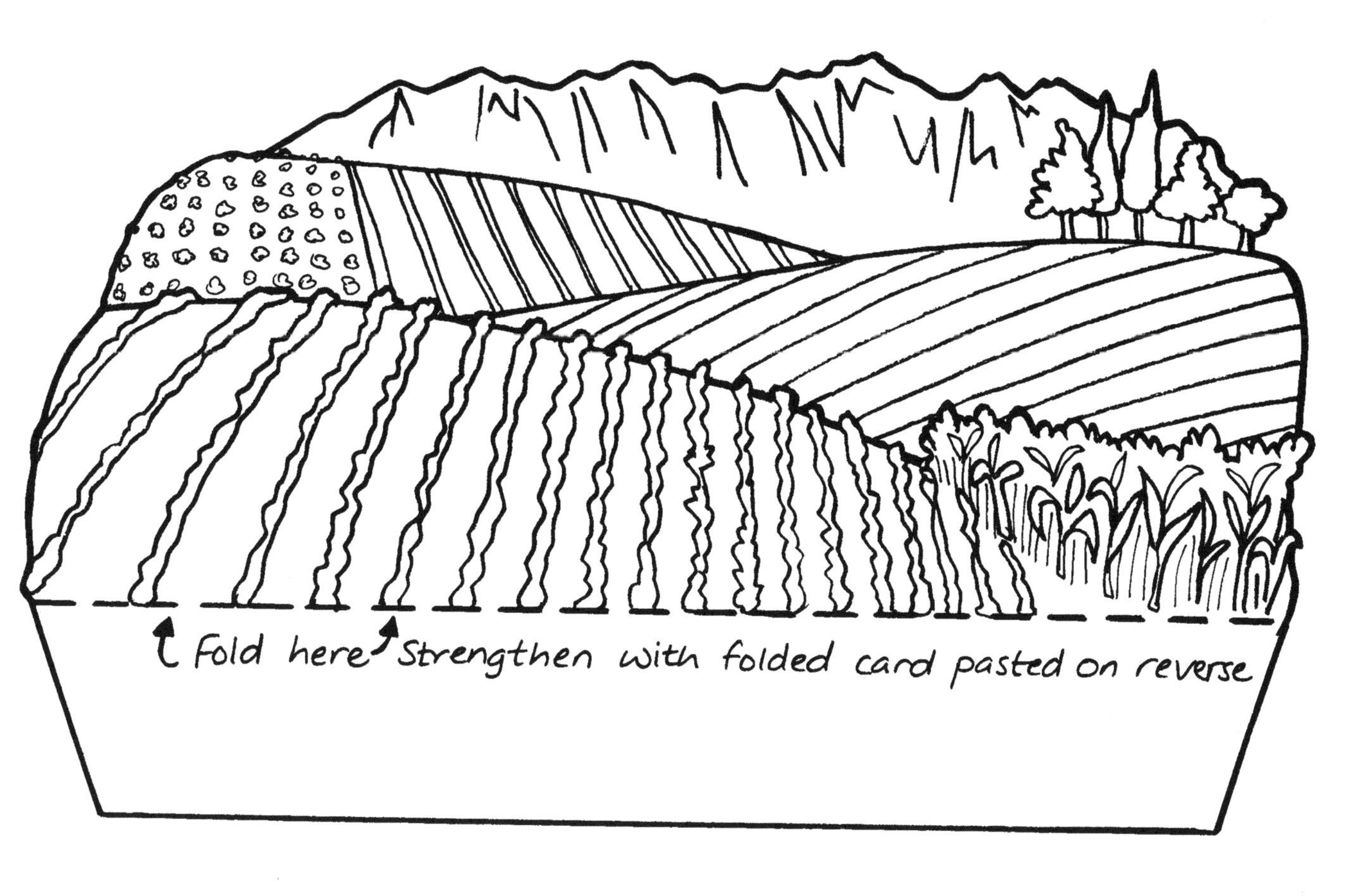
Fold here
Strengthen with folded card pasted on reverse

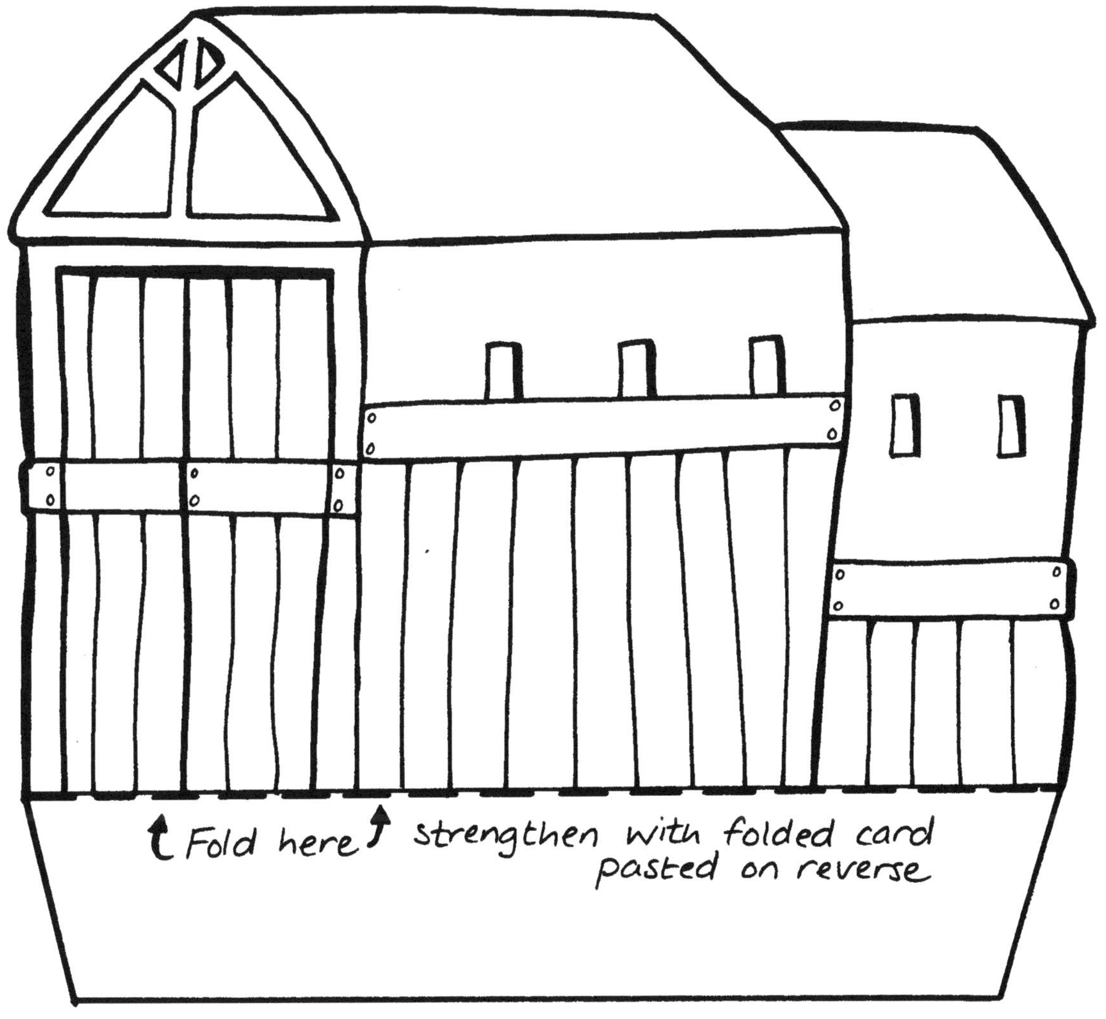
Fold here
strengthen with folded card pasted on reverse

The Sower

(Luke 8:4-8)

Cast

Farmer • Bird - ***this can be the "make". Stick feathers, fabric or paper onto the puppet with PVA glue to resemble feathers. You could make one for each child or get the children to do their own colouring or sticking.*** **• Plant • Sun • Thorny plant.**

The Sower

Stage directions

This is a story which Jesus told to his friends to explain to them that not everyone will follow God when they hear about him.

1. Farmer walks onstage going to and fro sowing seed (you can scatter some real seeds if you want to).

2. Farmer goes offstage.

One day a farmer (1) went out to sow some seeds. He had a bag full of seeds and he scattered them on the ground around him. He walked and he sowed and he walked and he sowed all day until all the seeds were sown. Then he went home for a rest (2). This story is about what happened to the seeds.

3. The bird puppet flies in and swoops several times over the ground.

4. The bird flies away.

Some fell on the path, and the birds (3) came and gobbled up those seeds - gobble, gobble, gobble. Jesus said that was like people who heard about God but then forgot all about God quickly. Jesus said that was like the birds snatching the seeds away and gobbling them up straight away rather than waiting for the seeds to turn into plants which would give the birds even more food (4).

Some of the other seeds fell on rocky places, which were all stony and dry. These seeds did grow into plants (5), and the plants grew up quickly, but when the hot sun (6) came up the plants dried up and died because they couldn't get any water (7). Jesus said that was like people who heard about God and were very happy to start with, but they didn't have any roots, things like Christian friends, praying, reading about God and going to worship God. So soon they stopped bothering about God.

5. The plant appears to grow (slowly draw the puppet up on its stick to full height).

6. The sun appears and rises into the sky.

7. The plant dies (drop the stick down) and the sun sets.

Some more of the seeds (8) fell among thorny plants. The seeds grew, but the thorny plants grew too, they grew quicker and bigger and thicker and tougher and thornier, and they choked the good plants (9). Jesus said that was like people who heard about God, but let other things become more important, so what God said wasn't important to them.

8. The plant grows again getting taller, and the thorn comes up too.

9. The plant and the thorn drop down.

And some of the seeds fell on good ground, where the soil was rich and damp and lovely for seeds to grow in (10). These seeds grew into plants and these

10. The plant comes up getting taller and taller.

plants grew taller and taller, and their roots got deeper and they grew into very good crops. Jesus said these seeds were like the people who heard about God, listened to God and who grew into strong Christians.

God loves us and wants us to be like the seeds that fell on the good ground.

Nutshell

God loves us and wants us to have good lives and to love God. If we love God then we will be like seeds growing in good ground.

Chatter Box

Have you ever sown some seeds and watched how they grow?

Can you imagine that you are a seed and God is watching you grow?

What kind of seed do you want to be?

Prayer Time

Thank you, God, for loving us.
Thank you, God, for all growing things.

Something to Do

Grow some seeds. Cress seeds are really quick and easy - you can grow them on damp paper in a bowl.

For "thorn" plant follow the same instructions as for "good" plant.
Fold Here
Strengthen with folded card pasted on reverse

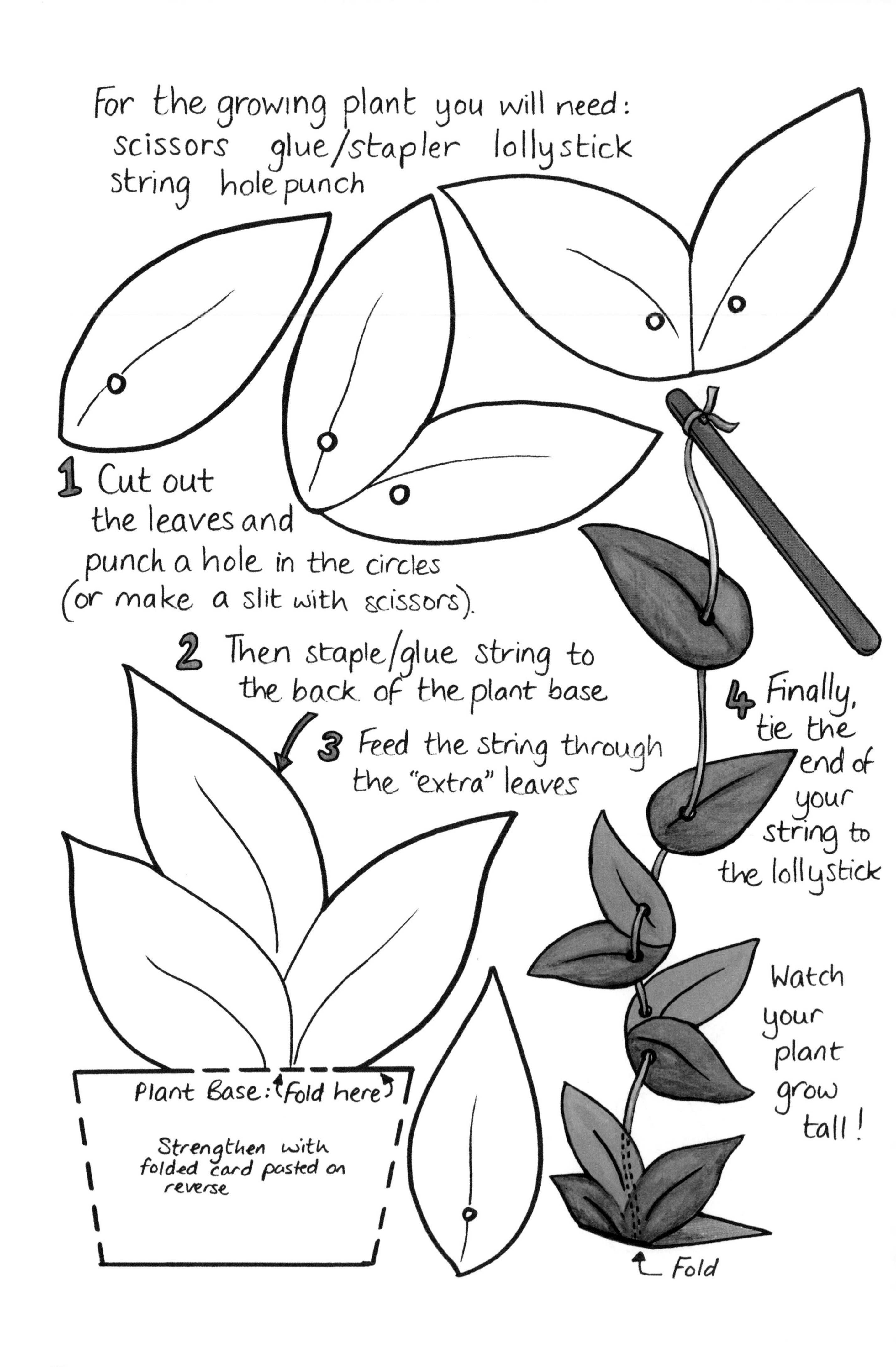
For the growing plant you will need:
scissors glue/stapler lollystick
string hole punch
1 Cut out the leaves and punch a hole in the circles (or make a slit with scissors).
2 Then staple/glue string to the back of the plant base
3 Feed the string through the "extra" leaves
4 Finally, tie the end of your string to the lollystick
Plant Base: Fold here
Strengthen with folded card pasted on reverse
Watch your plant grow tall!
Fold

The Grape Pickers

(Matthew 20:1-16)

Cast

The owner • First group of workers • Second group of workers • Third group of workers • Coins – *you will need all 3 identical puppets showing 3 coins on each* • Grapes – *this can be the "make". Stick green and red coloured circles onto the puppet, or colour them in. Make enough for all the children, then every time the narrator says "grapes" the children can hold their grape puppets up. Tell them this at the start of the show or the first time you say "grapes".*

The Grape Pickers

Stage directions

Jesus told this story to people to teach them more about heaven.

1. Owner of the fields walks to and fro across the stage.

2. The owner continues to walk and walks in among the grapes (all the children can hold theirs up).

There was a man (1) who owned great fields full of grape vines (2). They were very good fields and grew very good grapes, and the man made very good wine from the grapes.

Now one day he went to hire men to work in the fields. He needed them to hoe the weeds, trim the grape plants, and pick the grapes.

3. First group of workers onstage, the owner walks across to meet them.

He went to the town and there were some men (3) looking for work.

"Go to my fields, hoe the weeds, trim the grape plants and pick the grapes, and I will pay you a day's wages," he said. And the men went to the fields and they hoed the weeds, they trimmed the grape plants and they picked the grapes (4).

4. First group of workers go offstage.

Now the man who owned the fields of grapes went to town again later in the day (5), and there were some more men looking for work. So he said: "Go to my fields, hoe the weeds, trim the grape plants and pick the grapes, and I will pay you what is right." So the men went to the fields and they hoed the weeds, trimmed the grape plants and picked the grapes (6).

5. Second group of workers onstage, the owner walks across to meet them.

6. Second group of workers go offstage.

Later in the day the man went to town yet again (7), and there were still men looking for work. "Why are you men not working?" he asked. "No one has given us any work," they said. "Then go to my fields, hoe the weeds, trim the grape plants and pick the grapes," said the man (8).

7. Third group of workers go onstage, the owner walks across to meet them.

8. Third group of workers go offstage.

So the men went to the fields and they hoed the weeds and trimmed the grape plants and picked the grapes.

At the end of the day the owner of the grape fields (9) called all of the men who had been working, hoeing the weeds, trimming the grape plants and picking the grapes.

9. The owner walks among the grapes and is joined by all three groups of workers.

10. The coins appear and are given to each group

"Now I will pay you all," he said.

And he gave a day's pay (10) to each man. He gave a day"s pay to the men he had hired to work at the beginning of the day. He gave a day's pay to the men he had hired to work in the middle of the day. And he gave a day's pay to the men he had hired to work at the end of the day. All the men were given the same amount of money - one day's pay. The men looked at the money. Then the men who were hired to work at the beginning of the day said, "How can this be right? We have worked all day, hoeing the weeds, trimming the grape plants and picking the grapes, and some of these men have only worked a short time. Why do we all have the same amount of money for our work?" The men who had been hired to work in the middle of the day also grumbled a bit, and the men who had been hired to work at the end of the day kept very quiet.

Then the man who owned the grape fields spoke to them all.

"My friends, why are you grumbling? I offered you a day's pay for your work. You men who I hired to work this morning were offered a day's pay and you have been given a day's pay. I am a generous man, so I will pay the men who started work in the middle of the day a day's pay also. Maybe I am a very generous man, so those men who started work at the end of the day will also be paid a day's pay. So why do you complain? I am generous, and those who came late to work will have the same as those who came early, you should all be glad that I am a good man to work for, and you are all treated well."

Jesus told this story so that we would all know that God is generous and good. God gives us all the same and it doesn't matter if we are young or old, or when we come to know and love God.

Nutshell

God is generous like the man in the story. God chooses to give all of us the same life in heaven and not give less to people who have taken a long time to come to know and love God.

Chatter Box

Do you think the owner was good to everyone?

Do you sometimes feel people are not fair to you?

How does that make you feel?

Prayer Time

We thank you, God, that you are generous and good like the owner of the grape fields.
Help us to be generous and good to other people.

Something to Do

Share out some sweets or fruit equally with your friends or family – make sure everyone gets the same whether they are bigger or older or your best friend.

Fold here
Strengthen with folded card
pasted on reverse

Fold here
Strengthen with folded card
pasted on reverse

Fold here
Strengthen with folded card
pasted on reverse

The Old Woman Who Called in the Night

(Luke 18:1-8)

Cast

Old woman • Door - ***this can be the "make". Stick strips of brown paper on the puppet - you could make enough for all the children, so they can all knock each time. You could also create an opening door for the puppet show.*** **• Judge • Judge in nightclothes.**

The Old Woman Who Called in the Night

Stage directions

This was a story that Jesus told so that people would know how to pray to God.

1. Old woman walks onstage.

There was once an old woman (1). Her husband had died a long time ago, and so she lived all alone. She was not a happy old woman. She had an enemy who was not treating her fairly and that made her very unhappy. "I will go and speak to the judge," she said. "It is his job to make sure that I am treated fairly."

2. She reaches the door and knocks, getting louder each time (ask someone to make the knocking sounds by knocking on something like the underside of a table or chair).

So in the morning she went to the judge's house. She knocked on the door (2) - at first she knocked quite quietly, because the judge was a busy and important man, and she felt a little shy. She waited a while, but no one came to the door, so she knocked more loudly. Still no one came to the door, so she knocked even more loudly - knock, knock, knock.

3. The judge enters and they talk.

At last the judge (3) came to the door. "What do you want?" he asked.

"Good judge, I am sorry to bother you. I know you are busy and important, but I am being treated very unfairly and I am asking you to make things right."

"Ah, well. I see," said the judge. "These things can be tricky, and it might all take a long time. I'll see what can be done. But, umm, well..." (4)

4. The judge goes and the woman walks away.

So the old woman went home and waited for the judge to make things right.

5. The woman walks on again and knocks on the door, getting louder each time.

The next morning things still weren't right so she went to see the judge again (5). She knocked on the door - at first she knocked quite quietly, because the judge was a busy and important man, and she felt a little shy. She waited a while, but no one came to the door, so she knocked more loudly. Still no one came to the door, so she knocked even more loudly - knock, knock, knock.

6. The judge enters and they talk.

At last the judge (6) came to the door. "What do you want?" he asked.

"Good judge, I am sorry to bother you again. I know you are busy and important, but I am still being treated very unfairly and I am asking you to make things right."

"Ah, yes, well - I remember you came yesterday. As I said, these things can be tricky, very tricky, but I will see what I can do." (7)

7. The judge goes and the woman walks away.

So the old woman went home and waited for the judge to make things right.

The next morning things still weren't right, so she went to see the judge again. Now this time she didn't feel shy at all, (8) so she knocked loudly straight away, and the judge came to the door. (9) "Good judge, I am sorry to bother you" (she didn't say how busy and important the judge was, because now she was getting cross that he hadn't done anything for her) "but I am still being treated unfairly and I ask you to make things right."

8. The woman walks on again and approaches the door, she knocks once quite loudly.

9. The judge enters and they talk.

"Ah, yes, well - I will see what I can do, I'll really make an effort for you. You leave it with me and we should have things sorted by the end of the day," said the judge (10).

10. The judge goes and the woman walks away.

So the old woman went home and waited for the judge to make things right.

The morning passed, the afternoon passed, the day turned into evening, people were going to bed, and still she wasn't being treated fairly. So that night she went to see the judge again (11). She banged and banged and banged and banged very loudly on his door – knock, knock, knock!

11. The woman walks on again and approaches the door, she knocks so hard and loud that it falls down.

And the judge came to the door, all sleepy and wearing his nightclothes (12).

12. The judge appears in nightclothes, they talk, and the woman goes away jumping up and down.

"I am still being treated unfairly. You have a duty to make things right for me, and I have asked many times and now I ask again that you do your duty and make things right," said the old woman.

"Yes," said the judge, "you are right, I will make things right at once." The judge couldn't stand being bothered any more, especially not at night, because he liked peaceful nights and long sleeps. Now the old woman was treated right. She had justice, and she was happy, and she didn't need to bother the judge any more.

Jesus told the people this story so that they would know that if a lazy judge can be moved to listen to an old woman, then imagine how much better God is at listening to us. Because God always listens, and always answers our prayers, but not always in the way we expect and not always at the time we are expecting it to happen.

Nutshell

God is much better at listening to us than the judge in the story, but sometimes we need to be like the old woman and keep on asking God in prayer because God doesn't always answer prayer straight away. God doesn't mind how many times we ask for the same things!

Chatter Box

Do you sometimes have to ask for the same thing several times?

Do you always get what you have asked for?

Do you sometimes change your mind about what you really want?

Prayer Time

Thank you, God, that you listen to our prayers, and that you love to hear us when we pray. Help us to keep on praying and to get to know you better as we pray.

Something to Do

Play "whispers": whisper something very quietly to someone, if they don't hear then say it a little louder, and a little louder until they hear what you have said. Then let them have a turn.

fold here
Ask an adult to score along the thick line to make the door "open". You will need to glue some spare card to the door frame on the back to support it.

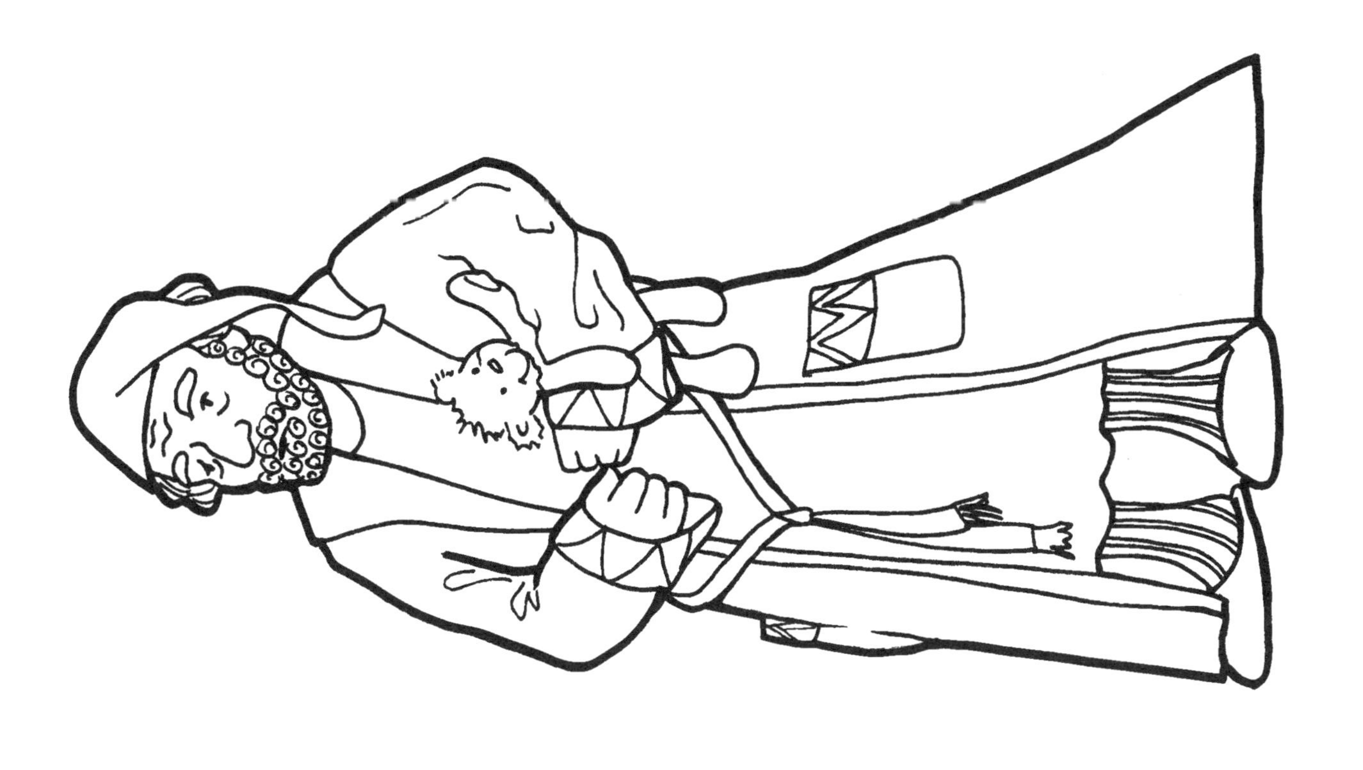

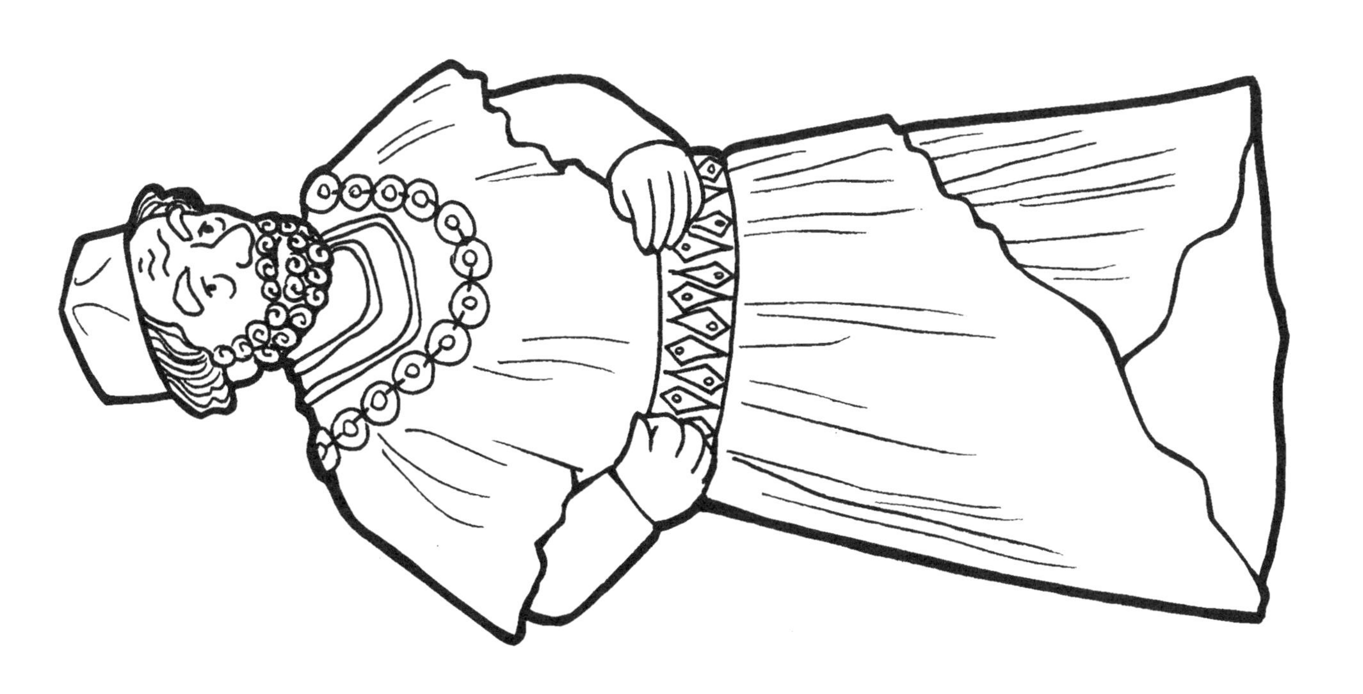

The Religious Man and the Tax Collector

(Luke 18:9-14)

Cast

Jesus • Group of people • Religious man • Temple interior • Tax collector • Coins - ***this is the "make". Cover the coin puppet with gold or silver foil; you can make one for each child and they can hold them up when the coins are mentioned.*** **• Food -** ***this can be an extra "make" and the children can hold them when the food is mentioned.***

The Religious Man and the Tax Collector

Stage directions

Jesus told this story to teach people to trust God and to teach them not to make judgements about who loves God best and to teach us all not to believe that we are always right (1). He sat down among a crowd of people and this is how he told the story:

1. Jesus talks to the group of people.

There were once two men. They were very different men (2). One was a very religious man – he went to the Temple a lot (3), and he prayed a lot. He also gave money to the Temple and he went without food sometimes, which made him feel hungry, but it also made him feel he was good.

2. The religious man walks on stage and Jesus and the group move off.

3. The temple interior puppet appears and the religious man walks beside it.

The other man was a tax collector (4). People didn't like him because of his job, which was to collect money for the government, and people often don't like paying money to the government – even now.

4. The tax collector walks on and stands further from the temple doorway.

The tax collector was a humble man - he knew he wasn't always good.

Now both men were in the Temple praying. The religious man was feeling very good. He felt very pleased with himself, and he stood up tall and proud, and prayed something like this:

"O God, I thank you that I am not like other people. I am not a bad man, a thief, or a tax collector, and I do not do wrong things." He said this in a very pleased, posh voice and looked down his nose at the tax collector. The religious man went on with his prayer:

"O God, I am a good man, and I am pleased that you see all my goodness. You, God, have seen how I give lots of money to the Temple." ("I give far more than that miserable tax collector," he thought, but he didn't say that in his prayer to God. And he thought about the money, how much he had given, (5) how bright and gold all the coins were.) Then he went on with his prayer:

5. Coins appear.

"And God, I go without food twice every week, which makes me hungry" (6). (Now he thought about all the good food he usually ate and he imagined a

6. Food appears.

big table covered with lovely food, but he didn't say anything about that in his prayer to God either.) It was very hard to stop thinking about the food, but he went on with his prayer:

"Yes, Lord, I go without all that good food which shows how good I am. Amen."

Then he finished his prayer and stood feeling very good about himself and he thought how pleased God must be (7).

7. Food and coins go offstage, religious man moves to the back of the stage, tax collector to the front.

The tax collector stood by himself. His head was bowed, and he began his prayer:

"God, please show me mercy because I am a bad man." He thought of all the wrong things he had done, and he felt how very wonderful God was (8).

8. Temple and men off. Jesus and the group go onstage.

So Jesus sat telling the story and the people sat listening. They could imagine the Temple, and they felt how very quiet it was (9). They could imagine the religious man and the tax collector, standing quite far apart. They felt how good the religious man felt about himself, and how bad the tax collector felt about himself. Jesus was quiet. He waited as the people thought about the two men in the Temple.

9. The religious man and the tax collector appear floating above ground level, as if in the group's imagination.

Then he looked up and said:

"God loves that tax collector! You see, the tax collector is humble; he knows he has done some bad things, but he is so sorry."

Someone in the crowd stood up. "Jesus," he said, "what about the religious man?"

"Ah, yes," Jesus answered, "God is not so happy with him!"

The man in the crowd stood up again: "But that man does good things - he goes to the Temple, he gives money, he goes without food."

Jesus answered: "Indeed he does all those things, but he does not see the wrong things that he does, and he does not come to God and ask to be forgiven. He thinks he is right and he is proud, so even the good things he does are spoiled."

Jesus said: "God is happy with people who are humble, people who know they have done wrong and are sorry. God is not so keen on people who are proud and full of themselves."

Nutshell

God loves us, whoever we are, but we all need to say sorry for the wrong things we do and we need to listen to God and not just to ourselves.

Chatter Box

Do you ever feel like the religious man, a bit proud and pleased with yourself?

Do you ever feel like the tax collector?

Do you know other people who are like the two men in the story?

Is it easier to be friends with someone like the religious man or someone like the tax collector?

Prayer Time

Please, God, help us to know when we have done wrong and to say sorry. Help us to be humble and not to think that we are better than other people.

Something to Do

Try looking down your nose, what can you see? Is it a good view? Now look up at the sky or out of the window as far as you can see. Isn't that a better view?

tax money
Fold here
Strengthen with folded card on reverse

Fold here ↑ Strengthen with folded card pasted on reverse

↑ Fold here ↑ Strengthen with folded card pasted on reverse

The Lost Son

(Luke 15:11-32)

Cast

Dad • Younger son • Elder son • Friends • Food • Younger son in rags • Younger son in fine clothing • Pig - *this can be the "make". Stick pre-cut patches of pink and brown on the pig puppets. You can make a pig for each child.*

The Lost Son

Stage directions

Jesus told this story to the people, to teach how God forgives us.

1. Dad and two sons appear onstage.

There was once a man who had two sons (1), and they all lived together running the farm and sharing things. They shared the work and they shared the fun and life was good.

2. The elder son moves offstage and the younger son and dad talk.

One day the younger son (2) said, "Dad, I'd like to have my share of the farm now. I would like my share in cash so that I can go out in the world and do what I want to do."

3. Dad goes offstage. The younger son walks along.

4. Younger son is joined by friends onstage, then the food appears and they all dance and jump up and down.

So his dad gave him his share in cash. And the younger son set off and went far away (3) to another country. He had a great time. He made lots of friends, and he paid for lots of parties (4) for all his new friends. He spent money on food and he spent money on wine. He paid for treats and good things for himself and his friends. They really liked that!

But after a while all the money was gone. There was no money left to buy food and wine and treats and good things. The new friends didn't like that at all. They left the younger son all alone (5). He was hungry (6), he wanted something to drink, his clothes were a mess, and he was lonely.

. All go offstage.

. The younger son in rags
oes onstage.

After a while he managed to get a job (7) looking after pigs for a farmer. This was a nasty, smelly job and it didn't pay very well. Sometimes he got so hungry he ate the pig food. Yuk! Things had never been worse. He thought to himself, "The people who work for my dad are better off than me now – they don't go hungry and thirsty, and they're not so lonely."

. The younger son is joined
y the pig.

So he decided to go home (8). When his dad saw him coming across the fields, he ran (9) and he ran, and he hugged his son (10) and he hugged him some more. And the younger son said, "Oh Dad! I've been so foolish! I did it all wrong, I took the money you gave me and I wasted it away, I shouldn't even be called your son any more."

. The younger son in rags
valks along slowly, dad
ppears at the other end of
he stage.

. The dad runs towards the
ounger son.

0. The dad and younger son
ug and jump up and down
nd hug again.

11. Dad stays onstage, younger son in rags goes offstage, the younger son in good clothes goes onstage, the food appears.

But his dad called the servants to bring the best clothes, the best food and the best drink (11). "We're going to have the best party ever!" said his dad.

12. The elder son walks onto the far end of the stage.

Now that was all great, but then the elder son (12) came in from his day's work on the farm. He heard the music, he smelled the food, he saw people dancing, and he found out that his little brother had come home. He was not pleased - in fact he was very cross, so cross that he would not go in to the party with the music and the food and the dancing. So his dad came over to him (13).

13. The elder son is joined by his dad and they talk.

"Now my son, come in and celebrate, hear the music, eat the food, have a dance - your brother has come home."

"No, Dad, I will not! All these years I have worked hard for you and been a good son to you and I've done everything you wanted me to do. You never gave a party for me, and now my little brother is back, and he's been really stupid, and you go to all this trouble. It's not fair!"

"My son," said his dad, "you have always been here with me and we have shared everything. Now your

4. Elder son and dad go to
›in the younger son by the
arty food, they talk and
ug.

little brother is back with us again, and we will rejoice that he is here and we will share everything together. And we will have a great party!"

So the elder son understood that his dad loved both the sons (14), and he was happy and they did go in to the party and they did have the best time ever.

Jesus told the people that God is like the kind old dad in the story, who forgives his son even when he's been really foolish. Even when we've been really foolish, God still loves us and wants us to be his children.

Nutshell

Whatever we do, God will always love us and forgive us, and will always want us to be his children.

Chatter Box

Do you think the younger son was a bit silly?

Have you ever done things that were really a bit silly?

What did your mum or dad say when they found out?

Prayer Time

Thank you for loving us so much.
Help us to love you and to love other people.

Something to Do

Give your mum or dad a big hug.

Fold here
Strengthen with folded card pasted on reverse

Fold here
Strengthen with folded card pasted on reverse

THE END